thisbookbelongsto:

ICECREAM

Color the ICE CREAM for Ryan and his friends!

Color the ice cream the color of your favorite icecream!

Help Ryan Find his icecream cone

Color Ryan and his ice cream when you are finished!

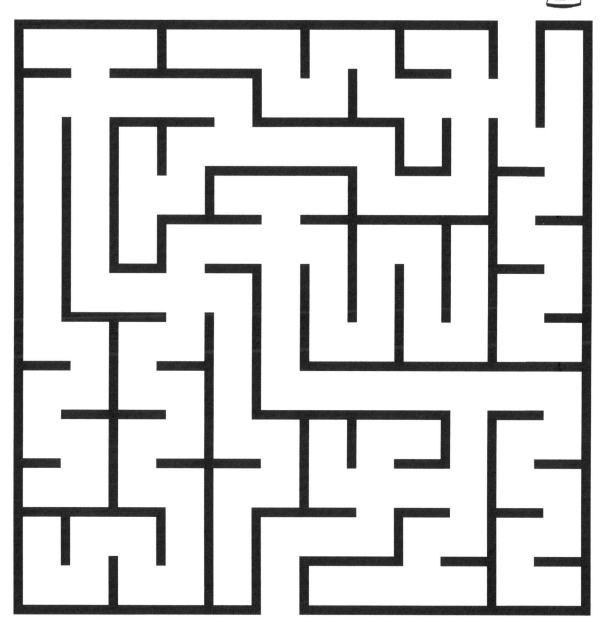

Color the ice cream cone!

Sweet complexion

Copyright © 2022 by Latrice English

All rights reserved. No part of this book may be reproduced, distributed,or transmitted in any form by any means, including photocopying, recording, or other electronic or mechanical methods, without the prior written permission of the author.

Printed in United States of America

Imprint: Independently Published
ISBN: 9798358739109
Publication Date:10/15/2022

Made in the USA
Monee, IL
02 February 2023

25986035R00015